AF264268

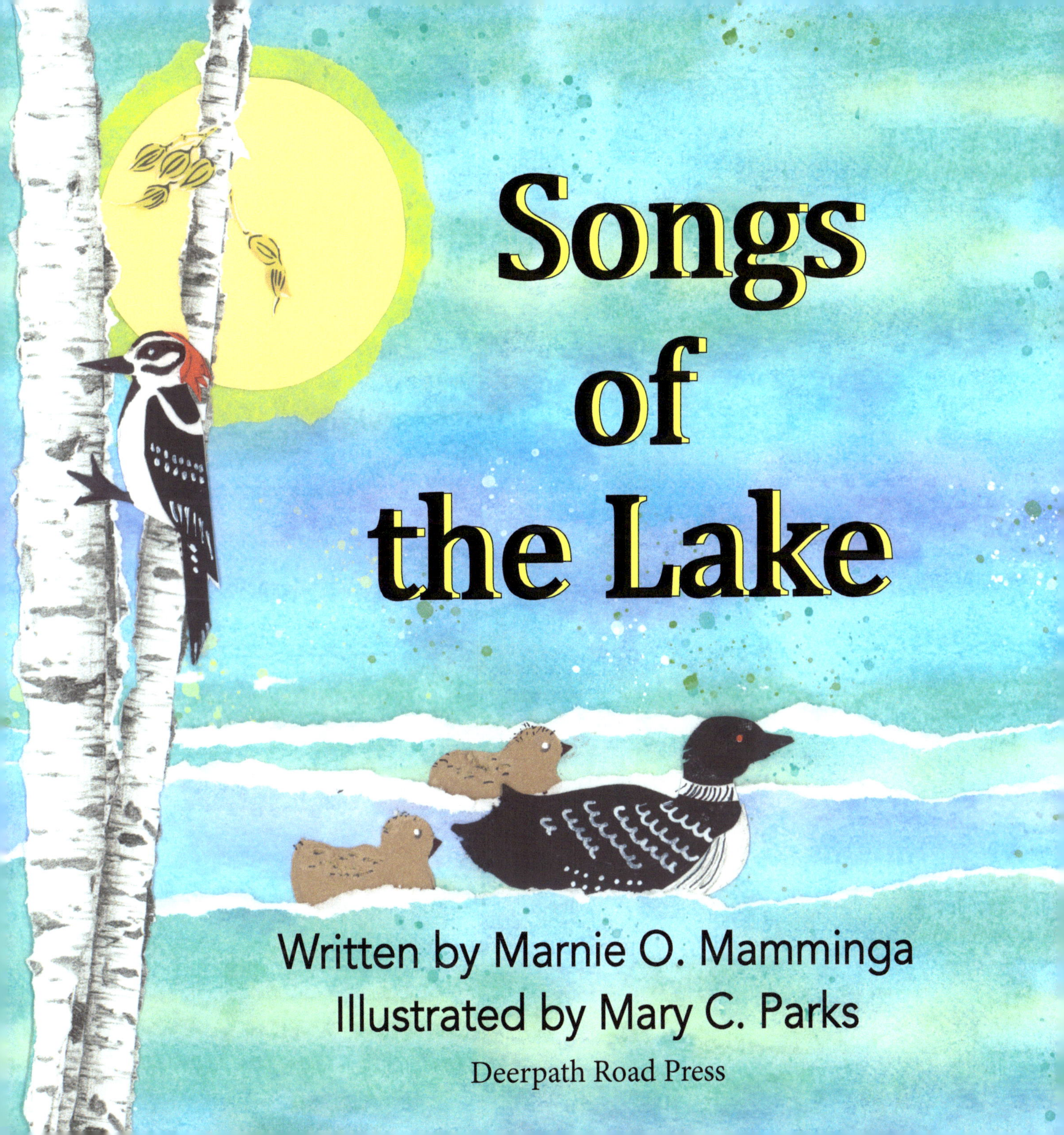

Songs of the Lake

Written by Marnie O. Mamminga

Illustrated by Mary C. Parks

Deerpath Road Press

Contact Marnie O. Mamminga and Mary C. Parks at marniemamminga.com

Publisher's Cataloging-in-Publication Data
Names: Mamminga, Marnie O., author. | Parks, Mary C., illustrator.
Title: Songs of the lake / Marnie O. Mamminga ; illustrated by Mary C. Parks.
Description: Batavia, IL: Deerpath Road Press, 2025.| Series: Finding wisdom in nature ; 3. | Includes 21 color illustrations. | Summary: A child discovers that sound carries over water and nature's melodies echo long after leaving the lake. |
Audience: 1-8 years.
Identifiers: LCCN 2025911911 | ISBN 9781966219187 (hardcover) | ISBN 9781966219194 (pbk.)
Subjects: LCSH: Nature – Juvenile fiction. | Sound – Juvenile fiction. | Summer – Juvenile fiction. | Lakes – Juvenile fiction. | LCGFT: Picture books. | BISAC: JUVENILE FICTION / Concepts / Sounds. | JUVENILE FICTION / Concepts / Seasons. | JUVENILE FICTION / Science & Nature / General.
Classification: LCC PZ7.1 M36 2025 | DDC [E]--dc22
LC record available at https://lccn.loc.gov/ 2025911911

Deerpath Road Press
Batavia, IL

In memory of my mother and father, who encouraged our family to listen for the sounds of nature on a Northwood's lake...

And to my sisters and brothers, Nancy, David, Tom, and Mary who continue to share the joy of nature together...

To my sons, John, Bob, and Tom, and daughters-in-law, Lara, Jennifer, and Rachel, who enthusiastically carry on the tradition...

To my beloved grandchildren, Marlo, Emmett, Alice, Ryan, Elena, Joy, Amber, and Lily, may you always hear and see nature's beauty...

And, of course, to Dave, whose voice I listen for everyday...

~ Marnie O. Mamminga

I dedicate my storyline illustrations for *Songs of the Lake* in loving remembrance and gratitude to my parents, George and Mary Gegeran. As a child, I fondly spent every summer of my life enjoying our summer home with three generations of families and friends on Leaf Lake in northern Minnesota.

It is my intent that my artwork in this book honors all nature's lakes and lands where people and all living things cohabit in peace.

~ Mary C. Parks

Together, we gratefully celebrate the two lakes that inspired us: Big Spider Lake, Hayward, Wisconsin, and West Leaf Lake, Ottertail, Minnesota.

"Hush!" my mother scolds. "Sound carries over water!"

Playing and splashing in the cold lake by our Northwoods cabin, my brothers and sisters and I have heard this warning many times before.

Even so, we always
forget to keep our
voices down.

Instead, my mother's frequent motto teaches us to *listen* for other sounds carrying over the water.

Usually, the sounds that catch
our attention first are like our own:

the shouts and laughter of
neighbor kids jumping off
their dock into cold water.

Sometimes, soft sounds
catch our ear: the gurgle of
a sailboat's tiller as the
bow plows through the
waves,

or the rhythmic drip of a paddle as our kayak
slides quietly through purple waterlilies in search
of a great blue heron,

or the low chatter of fishermen as their lures
plop one after another into still waters.

Othertimes, just the gentle whisper of wind through the trees speaks to us.

Most favorite, though, are the sounds of
the wildlife, their songs singing out to us in
happy abandon:

eagles chirping to their
chicks high in a nest,

owls hooting
through a moonlit forest,

or bullfrogs burping into
the early mist of the
dawn's rosy light.

But nothing speaks more to our hearts than the bell-like songs of loons in flight, the joyfulness of their music ringing across the sky.

I am always a little sad when
summer ends, for I will miss these
songs of the lake.

When nights are cold or days are dreary,
it is this symphony of music that
leads me back to the splendor
of sound carrying over water.

Lullabies
serenading me
to my dreams.

FUN FACTS

Did you know…?

1. The Great Blue Heron has a wingspan of 6 feet.

2. A Bald Eagle's Nest is called an eyrie and is made of large sticks. It can weight up to 2,000 pounds and lasts for many years.

3. Bull Frogs often sound like a cow mooing. They are the largest species of frog in the United States.

4. The Loons' flight song is called the tremolo. It is often called the "laughing call." Other calls of the loon are the yodel, the wail, and the hoot. All are used to communicate to other loons.

5. A Sailboat Tiller steers the boat. It is pushed in the opposite direction the sailor wants to go!

6. A Symphony is a long, beautiful piece of music written for many instruments. Listen to Mozart and Beethoven symphonies for some classic examples.

DISCUSSION QUESTIONS

1. What are some of the sounds or songs you hear in nature?

2. What are some of your favorite outdoor places to visit?

3. How do you feel when you leave a place you love?

4. How would you choose to remember a favorite place? Through a poem, art, photography, a song, or something else?

5. Which is your favorite illustration page? Why?

6. Which lake animal or person in the book did you like best?   Why?

7. What main colors do you see that remind you of summer?

Follow the magic circles...

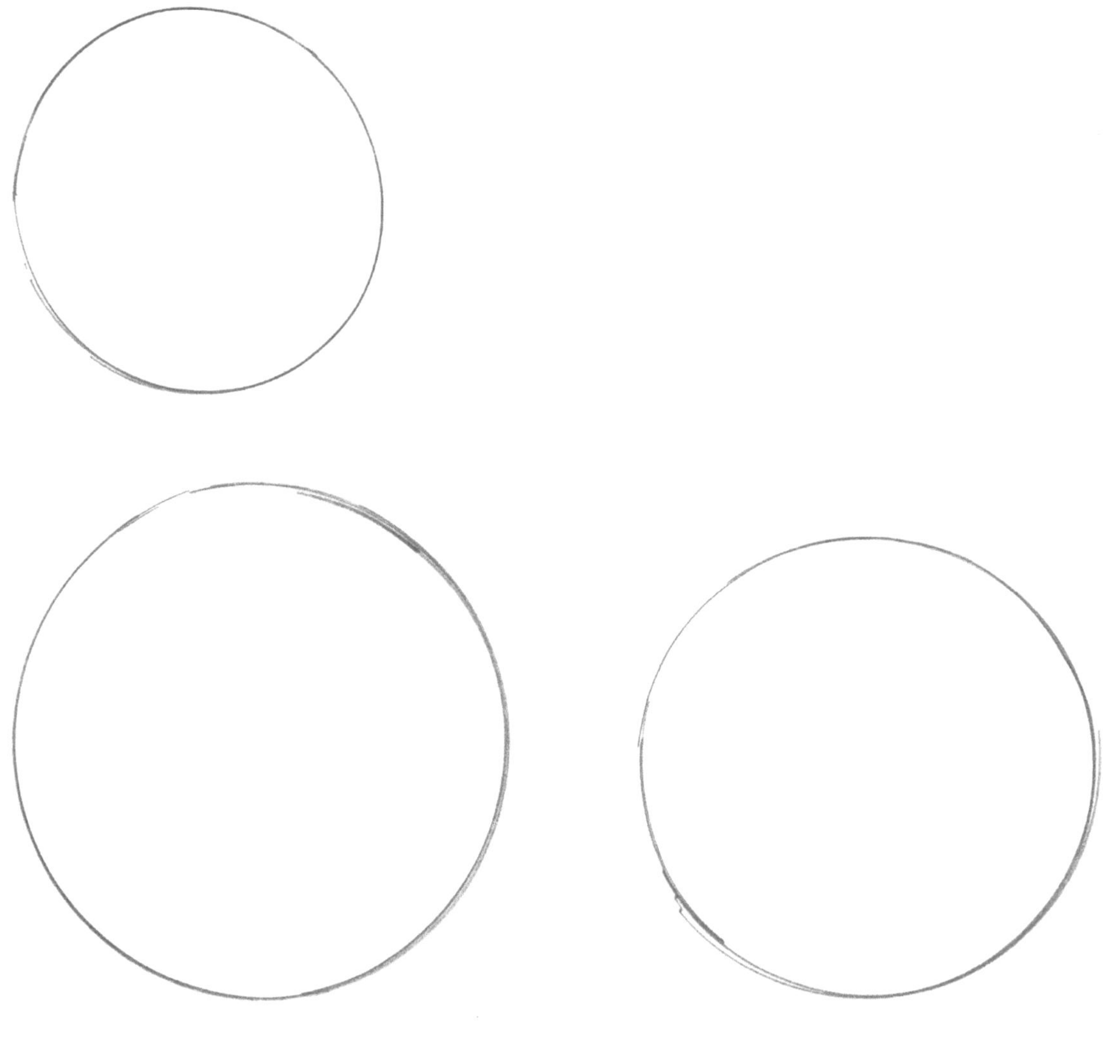

...to draw your own loon.

Meet the Author

Marnie O. Mamminga is the award-winning author of *Return to Wake Robin: One Cabin in the Heyday of Northwoods Resorts* and *On a Clear Night: Essays from the Heartland*. As a former educator, Marnie has also been a professional essayist and features writer for more than 30 years. Her work has been featured on NPR and in numerous regional and national publications, including the *Chicago Tribune*, *Reader's Digest*, *The Christian Science Monitor*, the *Midwest Prairie Review*, *Lake Superior Magazine*, *Detroit Free Press Magazine*, and in several *Chicken Soup for the Soul* books. In addition, she is a frequent perspective contributor for NPR's WNIJ.

The Woodpecker's Song, Mamminga and Parks' first children's book in their Finding Wisdom in Nature series, won two prestigious Eric Hoffer awards: Grand Prize Short List and First Runner Up in the Children's Category. *The Wolf Song in Me* is the second book in their song trilogy. Find out more about Marnie at marniemamminga.com. ~ **M.O.M.**

Meet the Illustrator

Mary C. Parks was born and raised in the suburban Midwest. These playful illustrations are intuitive to exploring the awe of summer family days and nights at the lake with her curious son, Brad, and grandsons, Anthony and Leo.

As a national and state acclaimed art teacher of thirty-five years, kindergarten through the college level, Mary also published her works in *ILLUSTRATOR* magazine for four years and illustrated several cookbooks. Retirement unfolded an unanticipated life for this multi-technique artist. While art history, travel, technology, and trends contribute, Mary's art echoes the spirit of her heartland roots.

"Art is the voice that uses no words; it sees, listens, and reflects. My illustrations for the *Songs of the Lake* were inspired by nature's glory and by reflecting on the enlightening words of author Marnie O. Mamminga. It is my hope that our words and illustrations awaken the imaginative wonder in the minds of children." ~ **M.C.P.**

Acknowledgments

Again, my heartfelt thanks…

To Sue Stephens for her enthusiastic acceptance of my NPR WNIJ perspectives from which this story sprang; to Gary King for his cheerful technical assistance and to Sammi King for our shared writing journeys; to Becky Hoag and the Batavia Public Library for inviting us to be a part of the legendary Books Between Bites program; to all the dear friends who have enthusiastically spread the word about our books; and to Christine Keleny of CKBooks Publishing for her patience, guidance, and expertise in making our dreams come true.

Most especially to Mary C. Parks, illustrator extraordinaire who not only brings amazing art to the page but does so with an intuitive wisdom and creative vision that continually surprises and delights. Her enchanting paper collage illustrations bring heartful joy to our shared Northwoods memories in *Songs of the Lake*.

To my sons, John, Bob, and Tom, and daughters-in-law, Lara, Jennifer, and Rachel, whose support and encouragement are always at the ready.

And, as always, to my husband Dave for all his behind-the-scenes efforts that continually ease the way on my writing journey.

~ Marnie O. Mamminga

When a writer possesses the talent to express words filled with visual imagery, an illustrator's mission is immediately sparked with enthusiasm to create. Thank you, Marnie, for inviting children and me outdoors to wander and to discover life's adventures on summer's northern lakes, perchance to hear the sounds and songs of the lake.

Thank you kindly for those who helped launch our books in our Finding Wisdom in Nature series: Christine Keleny of CKBooks Publishing, Colbert's Art Printing, Gary King, Becky Hoag, Batavia and Big Rock Libraries, Anderson's and Town House Bookstores, Naperville and Batavia School Districts, Beverly Shores Depot Museum and Art Gallery, IN, the many book presentation invitations, loving support of family and friends, our rock and unwavering encourager, Dave.

Gratitude to every child in my life that has conveyed to me their sense of discovery, wonder, and adventure, most directly my son, Brad, and my grandchildren, Anthony and Leo.

~ Mary C. Parks